Holly and Arthur leave school and turn at the corner. They find themselves in a dazzlingly lit street. "Look!" says Arthur. "Everyone has decorated their houses with amazing Christmas lights!" The street is glowing and magical. "There's Santa climbing into the chimney," calls Holly, pointing at the house in front of her. "And there are the kings!" Arthur shouts. "One... two... three!" Arthur stands very still next to them, pretending to be a fourth king. "I hope I get three gifts for Christmas," says Holly. "Me too," agrees Arthur. "But maybe not myrrh!"

Candy canes were first given out in Cologne Cathedral in Germany in 1670, but they didn't get their traditional red-and-white stripes until the 20th century.

Holly and Arthur arrive at the railway station to board a train into the city. "I can hear music," says Holly. "We sing this one at school," says Arthur. "It's all about a king who goes out into the cold to help someone looking for firewood." "How kind of him," replies Holly. "We should all remember to help others whenever we can." Among the crowd, Arthur spots a group of people carrying ice skates. "Quick, follow me!" he says, taking Holly's hand. "But Arthur—what about Aunt Clara's stocking?" Holly asks. "Don't worry. This won't take long," Arthur promises.

Arthur and Holly follow the crowd to an ice rink. "This is amazing!" shouts Arthur, who is trying to skate as fast as he can. Holly is practicing her swizzles. Suddenly, the Christmas lights go out. Arthur and Holly stop skating. "Oh no! They must have had a power cut," says Arthur. "That happened at home once, and we had to use candles. It felt like the olden days!" Around the sides of the rink, people start to sing. Gradually, more and more people join in. "This is beautiful," says Holly, looking up. "Who needs lights when you have a sky full of stars?"

On Christmas Eve in 1818, in a small village in the Austrian Empire, the melody for "Silent Night" was composed. It was accompanied by the guitar, as the church organ had been damaged.

In India, where there are no fir trees or pine trees, those who celebrate Christmas decorate mango trees or banana trees instead.

What's green, covered in tinsel, and says "Ribbet, ribbet"? A mistle-toad!

Holly and Arthur have made their way from the quiet ice rink to the city's bustling main square. Stalls are twinkling brightly, people are drinking mulled wine and hot chocolate, and in the middle is a huge tree covered in decorations. There is a juggler spinning five gold hoops in the air, and the crowd cheers every time he catches one. "He's juggling so fast that I can't count the rings," laughs Arthur. "I think there are five—just like in my favorite carol!" replies Holly. They play a quick game of *I Spy*, trying to find other items the carol sings about. "We'd better get going now if we want to make it to the store before it closes," says Arthur.

This carol is a cumulative song. That means that it starts with a simple verse that is added to, so that each new verse is longer than the one before it. Another famous cumulative song is "Old McDonald Had a Farm."

press here, little elves, this music goes from one to twelve!

In Oaxaca in Mexico, December 23 is "The Night of the Radishes." Christmas scenes are carved into big radishes and then displayed throughout the city.

Arthur and Holly are walking through the park to their favorite department store. It is snowing heavily now, and a cold wind is whistling through the trees. "It's really not that far," says Arthur. "It's just that the snow is really slowing us down." "In some parts of the world, where it snows all the time, people wear special snowshoes to help them get around more easily. They look a little like they have tennis rackets strapped to their feet!" Holly explains. Both giggle at the thought of this. Suddenly, they hear a bell chiming in the distance. "Oh no! We'll never make it!" Arthur exclaims. "We're almost there," Holly says, taking Arthur's hand. "I can see the lights up ahead."

Holly and Arthur have made it to the department store just in time! "Wow," says Holly, looking around. "I've never seen so many Christmas decorations!" There are shiny baubles and beads, glittering tinsel and tall trees, reindeer, and decorative wreaths. "Look—there are the stockings!" calls Arthur. "And stars. We need one of those for the top of the Christmas tree," replies Holly. They rush over to buy one of each. "Your aunt will be SO happy with us!" says Holly, carefully putting the gold star into her pocket. "And we've still got some money left over." So, Arthur picks himself a candy cane, while Holly chooses a slice of panettone.

In Costa Rica, the official flower of Christmas is the orchid.

What did the ocean say when Santa flew over it?
Nothing—it just waved!

Tired but happy, Arthur and Holly are walking home through the dark streets. They can see and hear carol singers going from door to door, delighting people with their festive tunes. "There's a girl in my class at school named Carol," says Holly. "She says it's because she was born at Christmas!" Arthur spots a snowman up ahead. "Good evening, Mr. Snowman," he says politely, replacing the snowman's carrot nose with a crayon from his pocket. "He's missing a button," says Holly, taking a candy from her coat and fitting it in place. "Much better." Across the street, the sound of an organ and singing is coming from an open church door. Holly and Arthur decide to go in…

The music for this carol was written by the French composer Adolphe Adam. He is most famous as the composer of the fantasy ballet *Giselle*.

In Caracas in Venezuela, it has become traditional to use roller skates on the streets between December 16 and December 24. The tradition is known as *las patinatas*.

Press the button if you desire, to hear a peaceful festive choir!

What do you sing at a snowman's birthday?

Inside the church, a carol service is taking place. The air is filled with a sweet, smoky scent, and candles are glowing along the aisles. Suddenly, a HUGE sound makes Holly and Arthur jump. They are standing right next to the church organ, and it has started playing VERY loudly. "My mom loves a carol service," says Holly. "She says it makes her feel like Christmas is truly here." They sit quietly and enjoy the choir's singing for a few minutes. Then Arthur leans over to Holly and whispers, "Speaking of moms, ours will be wondering where we've got to."

Freeze a jolly good fellow, freeze a jolly good fellow!

Press and music will appear, for you to "hark." (that means "hear.")

In the Netherlands, it is traditional for children to place their shoes or boots near the fire, so that Santa—or *Sinterklaas* as he's called in the Netherlands—can fill them with gifts. They also leave out a carrot—not for the reindeer but for Amerigo, the Christmas white horse!

It's late, and Holly is finally back at home. She plucks the gold star from her pocket and adds it to the top of the Christmas tree. "Perfect," her dad beams.

Down the street, Arthur is busy hanging stockings along the fireplace, including the one for Aunt Clara. "We'll put out a mince pie for Santa later," Arthur tells his sister. "We'll need a carrot for his reindeer, too!" she replies. Suddenly Arthur remembers his day. "I have just the thing!" He reaches into his pocket and finds a carrot. "Will a snowman's nose do the trick?"

Why was the turkey in the band? Because he was the only one with drumsticks!

Christmas Carol Lyrics

ONCE IN ROYAL DAVID'S CITY

Once in Royal David's city
Stood a lowly cattle shed
Where a mother laid her baby
In a manger for His bed
Mary was that mother mild
Jesus Christ her little child

He came down to Earth from Heaven
Who is God and Lord of all
And His shelter was a stable
And His cradle was a stall
With the poor, and mean, and lowly
Lived on Earth our Savior Holy

And through all His wondrous childhood
He would honor and obey
Love and watch the lowly maiden
In whose gentle arms He lay
Christian children all must be
Mild, obedient, good as He

For He is our childhood's pattern
Day by day, like us He grew
He was little, weak and helpless
Tears and smiles like us He knew
And He feeleth for our sadness
And He shareth in our gladness

And our eyes at last shall see Him
Through His own redeeming love
For that child so dear and gentle
Is our Lord in Heaven above
And He leads His children on
To the place where He is gone

Not in that poor lowly stable
With the oxen standing by
We shall see Him; but in Heaven
Set at God's right hand on high
Where like stars His children crowned
All in white shall wait around

WE THREE KINGS

We three kings of Orient are
Bearing gifts we traverse afar
Field and fountain
Moor and mountain
Following yonder star

O star of wonder, star of night
Star with royal beauty bright
Westward leading, still proceeding
Guide us to thy perfect light

Born a King on Bethlehem's plain
Gold I bring to crown Him again
King for ever, ceasing never
Over us all to reign

Frankincense to offer have I
Incense owns a Deity nigh
Prayer and praising
All men raising
Worship Him, God most high

O star of wonder, star of night
Star with royal beauty bright
Westward leading, still proceeding
Guide us to thy perfect light

Myrrh is mine: It's bitter perfume
Breathes a life of gathering gloom
Sorrowing, sighing, bleeding, dying
Sealed in the stone cold tomb

Glorious now behold Him arise
King and God and sacrifice
Al-le-lu-ia, al-le-lu-ia
Heaven to Earth replies

O star of wonder, star of night
Star with royal beauty bright
Westward leading, still proceeding
Guide us to thy perfect light

GOOD KING WENCESLAS

Good King Wenceslas looked out
On the feast of Stephen
When the snow lay round about
Deep and crisp and even
Brightly shone the moon that night
Though the frost was cruel
When a poor man came in sight
Gath'ring winter fuel

"Hither, Page, and stand by me
If thou know'st it, telling
Yonder peasant, who is he
Where and what his dwelling?"
"Sire, he lives a good league hence
Underneath the mountain
Right against the forest fence
By Saint Agnes' fountain"

"Bring me flesh and bring me wine
Bring me pine logs hither
Thou and I will see him dine
When we bear them thither"
Page and Monarch forth they went
Forth they went together
Through the rude wind's wild lament
And the bitter weather

"Sire, the night is darker now
And the wind blows stronger
Fails my heart, I know not how
I can go no longer"
"Mark my footsteps, good my Page
Tread thou in them boldly
Thou shalt find the winter's rage
Freeze thy blood less coldly"

In his master's steps he trod
Where the snow lay dinted
Heat was in the very sod
Which the Saint had printed
Therefore, Christian men, be sure
Wealth or rank possessing
Ye who now will bless the poor
Shall yourselves find blessing

SILENT NIGHT

Silent night, Holy night
All is calm, all is bright
Round yon Virgin, Mother and Child
Holy infant so tender and mild
Sleep in Heavenly peace
Sleep in Heavenly peace

Silent night, Holy night
Shepherds quake at the sight
Glories stream from Heaven afar
Heavenly hosts sing Alleluia
Christ the Savior is born
Christ the Savior is born

Silent night, Holy night
Son of God love's pure light
Radiant beams from Thy Holy face
With dawn of redeeming grace
Jesus Lord, at Thy birth
Jesus Lord, at Thy birth

THE TWELVE DAYS OF CHRISTMAS

On the first day of Christmas
My true love sent to me
A partridge in a pear tree

On the second day of Christmas
My true love sent to me
Two turtle doves
And a partridge in a pear tree

On the third day of Christmas
My true love sent to me
Three French hens
Two turtle doves
And a partridge in a pear tree

On the fourth day of Christmas
My true love sent to me
Four calling birds
Three French hens
Two turtle doves
And a partridge in a pear tree

On the fifth day of Christmas
My true love sent to me
Five gold rings
Four calling birds
Three French hens
Two turtle doves
And a partridge in a pear tree

On the sixth day of Christmas
My true love sent to me
Six geese a-laying
Five gold rings
Four calling birds
Three French hens
Two turtle doves
And a partridge in a pear tree

On the seventh day of Christmas
My true love sent to me
Seven swans a-swimming
Six geese a-laying
Five gold rings
Four calling birds
Three French hens
Two turtle doves
And a partridge in a pear tree

On the eighth day of Christmas
My true love sent to me
Eight maids a-milking
Seven swans a-swimming
Six geese a-laying
Five gold rings
Four calling birds
Three French hens
Two turtle doves
And a partridge in a pear tree

On the ninth day of Christmas
My true love sent to me
Nine ladies dancing
Eight maids a-milking
Seven swans a-swimming
Six geese a-laying
Five gold rings
Four calling birds
Three French hens
Two turtle doves
And a partridge in a pear tree

On the tenth day of Christmas
My true love sent to me
Ten lords a-leaping
Nine ladies dancing
Eight maids a-milking
Seven swans a-swimming
Six geese a-laying
Five gold rings
Four calling birds
Three French hens
Two turtle doves
And a partridge in a pear tree

On the eleventh day of Christmas
My true love sent to me
Eleven pipers piping
Ten lords a-leaping
Nine ladies dancing
Eight maids a-milking
Seven swans a-swimming
Six geese a-laying
Five gold rings
Four calling birds
Three French hens
Two turtle doves
And a partridge in a pear tree

On the twelfth day of Christmas
My true love sent to me
Twelve drummers drumming
Eleven pipers piping
Ten lords a-leaping
Nine ladies dancing
Eight maids a-milking
Seven swans a-swimming
Six geese a-laying
Five gold rings
Four calling birds
Three French hens
Two turtle doves
And a partridge in a pear tree

CAROL OF THE BELLS

Hark! how the bells
Sweet silver bells
All seem to say
"Throw cares away"
Christmas is here
Bringing good cheer
To young and old
Meek and the bold

Ding, dong, ding, dong
That is their song
With joyful ring
All carolling
One seems to hear
Words of good cheer
From ev'rywhere
Filling the air

Oh how they pound
Raising the sound
O'er hill and dale
Telling their tale
Gaily they ring
While people sing
Songs of good cheer
Christmas is here
Merry, merry, merry, merry Christmas
Merry, merry, merry, merry Christmas

On, on they send
On without end
Their joyful tone
To ev'ry home

Hark! how the bells
Sweet silver bells
All seem to say
"Throw cares away"
Christmas is here
Bringing good cheer
To young and old
Meek and the bold

Ding, dong, ding, dong
That is their song
With joyful ring
All carolling
One seems to hear
Words of good cheer
From ev'rywhere
Filling the air

Oh how they pound
Raising the sound
O'er hill and dale
Telling their tale
Gaily they ring
While people sing
Songs of good cheer
Christmas is here
Merry, merry, merry, merry Christmas
Merry, merry, merry, merry Christmas

On, on they send
On without end
Their joyful tone
To ev'ry home

JOY TO THE WORLD

Joy to the world! the Lord is come
Let Earth receive her King
Let every heart prepare him room
And Heaven and nature sing
And Heaven and nature sing
And Heaven, and Heaven, and nature sing

Joy to the world! the Saviour reigns
Let men their songs employ
While fields and floods, rocks, hills, and plains
Repeat the sounding joy
Repeat the sounding joy
Repeat, repeat the sounding joy

No more let sins and sorrows grow
Nor thorns infest the ground
He comes to make His blessings flow
Far as the curse is found
Far as the curse is found
Far as, far as, the curse is found

He rules the world with truth and grace
And makes the nations prove
The glories of His righteousness
And wonders of His love
And wonders of His love
And wonders, wonders, of His love

O HOLY NIGHT

O Holy night, the stars are brightly shining
It is the night of the dear Saviour's birth
Long lay the world in sin and error pining
'Til He appeared and the soul felt its worth
A thrill of hope the weary world rejoices
For yonder breaks a new and glorious morn

Fall on your knees
O hear the angel voices
O night divine!
O night when Christ was born
O night, O Holy night, O night divine

Led by the light of Faith serenely beaming
With glowing hearts by his cradle we stand
So, led by light of a star sweetly gleaming
Here come the wise men from Orient land
The King of Kings lay thus in lowly manger
In all our trials born to be our friend

He knows our need, To our
weakness no stranger
Behold your King! Before
Him lowly bend
Behold your King! Your King!
Before Him bend

Truly He taught us to love
one another
His law is Love and His gospel is Peace
Chains shall He break, for
the slave is our brother
And in His name all oppression
shall cease
Sweet hymns of joy in
grateful Chorus raise we
Let all within us praise his Holy name

Christ is the Lord, then ever! Ever
praise we
His pow'r and glory, evermore
proclaim
His pow'r and glory, evermore
proclaim

HARK! THE HERALD ANGELS SING

Hark! The herald angels sing
"Glory to the newborn King!
Peace on earth and mercy mild
God and sinners reconciled"
Joyful, all ye nations rise
Join the triumph of the skies
With th'angelic host proclaim
"Christ is born in Bethlehem"
Hark! The herald angels sing
"Glory to the newborn King!"

Christ by highest Heav'n adored
Christ the everlasting Lord
Late in time behold Him come
Offspring of a Virgin's womb
Veiled in flesh the Godhead see
Hail the incarnate Deity
Pleased as man with man to dwell

Jesus, our Emmanuel
Hark! The herald angels sing
"Glory to the newborn King!"

Hail the heav'n-born Prince of Peace
Hail the Son of Righteousness
Light and life to all He brings
Ris'n with healing in His wings
Mild He lays His glory by
Born that man no more may die
Born to raise the sons of Earth
Born to give them second birth
Hark! The herald angels sing
"Glory to the newborn King!"

WE WISH YOU A MERRY CHRISTMAS

We wish you a merry Christmas
We wish you a merry Christmas
We wish you a merry Christmas
And a happy New Year

Good tidings we bring to you
and your kin
We wish a merry Christmas
and a happy New Year
Now bring us some figgy pudding
Now bring us some figgy pudding
Now bring us some figgy pudding
Now bring some out here

Good tidings we bring to you
and your kin
We wish you a merry Christmas
and a happy New Year
For we all like our figgy pudding
For we all like our figgy pudding
For we all like our figgy pudding
With all this good cheer

Good tidings we bring to you
and your kin
We wish you a merry Christmas
and a happy New Year
And we won't go until we get some

And we won't go until we get some
And we won't go until we get some
So bring some out here

Good tidings we bring to you
and your kin
We wish you a merry Christmas
and a happy New Year
We wish you a merry Christmas
We wish you a merry Christmas
We wish you a merry Christmas
And a happy New Year

Did you spot the gingerbread man?

Did you spot George the gingerbread man hiding on the pages of this book? If so, well done! If you didn't, why not look again now—he appears 10 times.

Answers: **Once in Royal David's City:** On the stage. **We Three Kings:** On the garden wall. **Good King Wenceslas:** In the crowd on the platform. **Silent Night:** Skating by the Christmas tree. **The Twelve Days of Christmas:** Under the Christmas tree by the steps. **Carol of the Bells:** Under the flowers. **Joy to the World:** In the basket of toys. **O Holy Night:** Among the carol singers. **We Wish You a Merry Christmas:** At the table at Holly's house. **Hark the Herald Angels Sing:** Under the organ bench.

Acknowledgements

Published by Dorling Kindersley Ltd in association with Classic FM, part of Global Media and Entertainment Group Ltd. "Once in Royal David's City," "Silent Night," "Carol of the Bells," "Joy to the World," "O Holy Night," and "Hark! The Herald Angels Sing" licensed courtesy of Naxos Music UK Limited. "We Wish You a Merry Christmas" licensed courtesy of Avie Records. "The Twelve Days of Christmas licensed courtesy of The Gift of Music. "We Three Kings of Orient Are" and "Good King Wenceslas" licensed courtesy of Musical Concepts.

"Carol of the Bells" By Peter J. Wilhousky. Copyright © 1936 by Carl Fischer, Inc. Copyright renewed. All rights assigned to Carl Fischer, LLC. All rights reserved. Used with Permission.

Text copyright © Tim Lihoreau and Philip Noyce, 2024

Artwork copyright © Sally Agar, 2024

Project Editor Vicky Armstrong
Senior Designer Clive Savage
Designer Andrew Watson
Production Editor Siu Yin Chan
Senior Production Controller Louise Minihane
Senior Acquisitions Editor Katy Flint
Managing Art Editor Vicky Short
Publishing Director Mark Searle

First American Edition, 2024
Published in the United States by DK Publishing,
1745 Broadway, 20th Floor, New York, NY 10019

Page design copyright © 2024 Dorling Kindersley Limited
DK, a division of Penguin Random House LLC

24 25 26 27 28 10 9 8 7 6 5 4 3 2 1
001–338172–Sep/24

All rights reserved. Without limiting the rights under the copyright reserved above, no part of this publication may be reproduced, stored in or introduced into a retrieval system, or transmitted, in any form, or by any means (electronic, mechanical, photocopying, recording, or otherwise), without the prior written permission of the copyright owner. A catalog record for this book is available from the Library of Congress.
ISBN: 978-0-5938-4394-9

DK books are available at special discounts when purchased in bulk for sales promotions, premiums, fund-raising, or educational use. For details, contact: DK Publishing Special Markets, 1745 Broadway, 20th Floor, New York, NY 10019
SpecialSales@dk.com

Printed and bound in China

www.dk.com

This book was made with Forest Stewardship Council™ certified paper—one small step in DK's commitment to a sustainable future. Learn more at www.dk.com/uk/information/sustainability